Life
After The Pain

By Yung Muusik Randall

Copyright

Copyright © 2023

All Rights Reserved

Publisher: The Mason Publishing Company

This Book contains privacy of the author you cannot copy or duplicate this book all rights reserved. No part of this publication may be reproduced, stored in a retrieval system, or transmitted in any form or by any means -electronic, mechanical, photocopy, recording, or any other- except for brief quotations in printed reviews, without the prior permission of the publisher. For information address:

Themasonpublishingcompany2020@gmail.com

printed in the United States of America

ISBN: 979-8-218-96976-9

Table of Contents

Title Page

Copyright Page..1

Table Of Contents..2

Acknowledgements..4

Dedication..5

Introduction...6

Chapter 1 The Projects..8

Chapter 2 Growing up without a father.................11

Chapter 3 Foster Child..14

Chapter 4 Living with Granny.................................17

Chapter 5 Church Boy...20

Chapter 6 Trouble Boy..22

Chapter 7 Mom going to prison.............................25

Chapter 8 Shadows of Death..................................27

Chapter 9 Set Up...32

Chapter 10 Solo …………………...........................36

Chapter 11 Falling Deep in Love …………..………39

Chapter 12 Domestic Violence………………………….43

Chapter 13 Custody Battle……………………………50

Chapter 14 Single Father……………………...............54

Chapter 15 Gotta Do Something ………………...62

Chapter 16 The Industry…………………………….......65

About The Author (BIO)……………………….……70

Yung Muusik & Industry Friends…………………......73

Yung Muusik & Family……………………………...80

Pursuit of Success………………………………..88

Yung Mussik Award Winnings…………………….93

Yung Power Foundation………………………………95

Consistency Is Key……………………………….97

Believe……………………………………………......98

Keep The Faith……………………………………99

Acknowledgments

I want to give thanks to God for allowing me to do all that I am doing in my life today, I also want to thank my mom and my grandmother for just really believing in me and to The Mason Publishing Company for also believing in me and helping me on my book journey making it all possible I really appreciate everything.

Dedication

I dedicate my book to GOD FIRST because of Him, He made it all possible. To my kids Aniya Randall & Samar Randall Daddy love yall with all of me and I wouldn't trade it for nothing in this world. To my mother and my granny thank yall for believing in me on my next journey in being an Author. I also dedicate this book to myself for being the strong individual that has been through it all and is still alive to talk about it. Finally, to the people all over the world no matter how bad it gets keep going for what you believe and trust that GOD WILL MAKE A WAY FOR YOU, continue to keep the Faith.

Introduction

My life has been like a roller-coaster one minute I was up and the next minute I was down but through it all I remained strong I had to. I had to show up for myself and be the man that I knew I could be and that's ambitious and a man of Faith. For every struggle there is a way out even when at that very moment you can't see no way out, just know that there is one. I didn't choose the cards that I have been dealt with when I was younger, but as I got older, I've learned to choose how I handled life decisions, I've realized that not every move that we make or every choice in life will be perfect to me it's all a lesson. I hope that my story inspires you along the way.

Chapter 1

The Projects

Growing up in the projects taught me a lot of things, living with my granny in a house full of ten, she was always on us about going to school, keeping God first and making sure that we said our prayers before we walked out that door. Granny always made sure that we kept in mind that a bullet didn't have any name on it. Just thinking back to when I was six years old, I heard my very first gunshots. It had me kind of scared, I didn't know what was going on. All I know is I heard screaming, yelling and gunshots. All I could do was drop to the floor. All I heard was "everybody gets down! me, this six-year-old boy, frightened, scared, didn't know what to do and sure didn't know what was going to happen next. As everything cleared up, I can remember like it was yesterday, me and my cousin got up from off the floor and we opened up the living room door. I went outside first, and my cousin followed behind me, he was much older than I was, but I was very smart for my age, and I was very aware of my surroundings. I was standing outside in disbelief. I couldn't believe my own eyes. I was traumatized. This six-year-old boy witnessed my first crime scene, there was a guy lying there shot multiple times there was blood everywhere on the ground. The guy was still breathing as I saw him get picked up by the ambulance. He was alert. All the neighbors were standing outside, even after the ambulance had left. Everyone stood around and talked about the incident while me and my cousin went back into the house. Living in the projects was tough, but after living there for so many years my grandmother decided to move us out of there. With all the gang violence and police brutality that was going on, this had to be her last straw, it was time for us to move. For anybody who knows it surely was granny who knew what was best for us and I'm thankful that she made the right decision.

Chapter 2

Growing up without a father

It was December 25th, 1987, on Christmas day my mom was only 16 years old giving birth to her first-born son, who? me. What a coincidence that I was born on a special holiday. I remember my mom telling me the story of how she held me in without going into labor so I could be a Christmas baby. I always laugh when I think about that story because I am A gift, at least I believe so. My father was present at the time of my mom's delivery, he had to be because he signed the birth certificate. Unfortunately, he wasn't around in my life growing up.

My mom and my family on my dad's side used to tell me stories about him, which were some crazy stories that made me kind of afraid to meet him as I got older. My father was gang affiliated. He was in and out of jail, he had a reputation and still to this day he does.

Every boy needed their father in their life as a child to show and teach them things that a boy needed to be taught. Like how to protect myself, how to push me to my full potential, how to stand up for myself, and to teach me how to become a man, give me those one-on-one talks on how to treat a lady. With him not being there for me. I had to teach myself. During my pre-teens I struggled hard with my mom, we didn't have it all like that, I grew up on food stamps, but don't get me wrong my mom had many hustles, which led her to prison for 4 years. She got caught up in trying to make a way for me, my brothers and sister. Her only focus was to make ends meet and to make sure that we were good. At that very moment that's when I knew I had to grow up fast. I had to be the one to step in her shoes and become the one to look after them. The pressure was heavy on me because I couldn't see my mom in prison like that but what other choice did, I have? I couldn't do anything about it besides doing what I had to do.

Chapter 3

Foster Child

After my mom got sent off to prison, my whole world felt like it went upside down, I couldn't understand why, like for real why my mom? I was young but I remember it like it was yesterday. All I saw was police escorting me, my siblings, and my cousins out of the house. All you heard was screaming, my cousins started running from the police. It was a house full of us, this is what I saw. I saw my uncles getting slammed into the police car. I didn't know what to do. I was confused, sad, mad watching how everything unfolds in front of my eyes. I still don't know the story of how all of this took place. After all of the commotion my situation changed, I still couldn't believe I woke up in a stranger's home, a place called the foster system. I cried almost every day. I just wanted to go home, this was something I couldn't dare get used too, I missed my mom, my sister and brothers, I missed my family.

I was in the foster system for about a month, but it felt like a whole year. I was placed in different homes. Off the top of my head, I can only remember two. I would go and visit my granny, we used to meet up at McDonalds. When it was time to leave, I hated to go. Being that young it was a lot to take in at the time, but I did receive good news that my mom had gotten released from prison.

Chapter 4

Living with Granny

Despite the foster system I had a granny that fought hard to do what she had to do to take us in, and to become full guardianship over me and my sister and brothers. My granny took 5 of us in yall know how granny does it. There's no limit to the love that she gives. My mom was pregnant while in prison and after she gave birth, my grandmother went and brought the baby home. Granny had a house full where you had to get in where you fit in. The living room was where I slept. I was just happy to be there and not living in the system.

My Granny didn't live in the greatest neighborhood, the neighborhood where I'm talking about gangstas, drug dealers, killas, hookahs, you name it, and it was there. It was kind of tough living in that neighborhood. My granny opened her door to family, and friends, she was just that type of person. She would cook breakfast and we ate dinner early. She kept us in church. That's what I loved about her. I learned a lot from my granny as far as keeping the house clean and keeping up my hygiene and even learned how to cook. Well, my cooking skills came from my mom and my granny. They both were great cooks. I was young but being in my environment wasn't the best, it was easy for me to fall victim to my society.

Chapter 5

Church Boy

Being brought up in church for me was more like a blessing and a curse. I felt that way because when I wanted to do good there was always something trying to get in the way of that and caused me to do things, I knew I shouldn't be doing, say for instance hanging around the wrong crowd. Everything was glorified by the church, but in reality, I wanted to be a gangsta. My mom and my dad were gangstas, that's all I knew. I was a teenager. I was fighting every day on the block, breaking into cars, stealing out of stores. This was my way of survival. I never really got put on, but I did gain respect from the OGs. They even gave me a nickname they used to call me sneak loc, I used to be really quiet but with the business. I even got shot at. I even shot at people. While I was affiliated with the streets, I still attended every church meeting, I was in every church play, I was on the praise team, I was even the goddamn easter bunny on resurrection day. I was like man I got to be the bunny really, out here passing out eggs.

I'm just blessed that I didn't get caught up like a lot of my friends did. I guess putting God first in spite of everything paved a way for me and He kept his hands over my life.

Chapter 6

Trouble Boy

I had this pretty boy swag type of look, which mistaken my kindness for weakness. My looks didn't change my behavior. I was acting out of disobedience. I had to look out for myself, so it wasn't anything pretty about me when it came to me having to defend myself. I've really had to put up this wall after hearing about one of my everyday friends getting shot in the head. He was only fourteen. This was close to home for me so being that I was about his age I knew that a bullet didn't have any name on it. That really opened my eyes but then again it didn't. In the streets I was taught to be careful how you move. I remember I used to throw rocks at cop cars, break windows, all types of crazy shit I didn't care about nothing. I was a boy doing what boys without no guidance do. The girls that were my age always crushed on me, even some of the older women too. When I would go visit my cousin in Ontario California for the summer, we would always be around the ladies. I would even get flirted with by their mommas, at least that was my impression. I used to call myself a pimp and did not even know the definition behind it. I used my talents, my singing and rap battles to wheel them in. I was like 12 hanging around 14-, 15-, 16-, and 17-year-olds even ages 21. I always lied about my age; it wasn't anything sexual involved that wasn't my main focus. The things that I had to face every day in the streets by me being the youngest I always expressed myself with my talents and that also attracted people around me such as close female friends and some of my close homies. I was considered bad but if you knew me when I was younger you wouldn't think that about me because I was very sneaky and didn't allow people in my business.

Chapter 7

Mom going to prison

A lot of my upbringing by how I behaved growing up, I believe it had a lot to do with the absence of both my parents. Far as being in and out of jail. Even though my granny raised me it's nothing like having your parents in your life and I feel I was robbed of that. My mom taught me a lot, she was a single mom, and she was the type of mom that was a true hustler. My mom was 16 when she had me, she was a kid having a kid. So pretty much it wasn't nothing that she wouldn't do for us even if she had to scam, rob, steal, she didn't give a fuck. If I think about it, she was only doing what any mother would have done to make sure her kids didn't go without. I might not have understood it when I was growing up but now that I'm older I take my hat off to her and give her props for that. I've learned a lot from that situation as far as being in the streets myself as a young adult the only difference is I could say I'm street smart and book smart it gave me the best of both worlds which I still use as of today.

Chapter 8

Shadows of Death

I lived in Compton; I would always have my cousin come and visit me, we were super close and at a young age we always had something up our sleeves when we would visit each other. When he would come to Compton, we would always hit a few corners and get into some shit far as socking somebody off their bike, high jacking a car, bust out moving car windows we would stand on the street and throw big ass rocks at cars. Or we would go into the corner store and steal all types of shit. My cousin he lived in Ontario Ca, so we would pretty much go back and forth to each other houses but it never fails when we link up because we knew that we were going to be up to know good, it's like we had got of kick out of doing some crazy shit.

 I remember one night while visiting my cousin we walked to go pick up one of our friends who also stayed in the same complex as my cousin. When we got there, we all decided to take a walk to the store but on the way to the store it was a busy street. My cousin was like let's throw rocks at the cars, so I was like I'm with it lets do it. So, we are throwing rocks here and there and my cousin picked up this big ass boulder rock, and we said the next car that rides by we just gone throw that shit at it. The next car that came by was a van and next thing, you know, we did exactly what we said we were going to do, we picked up the rock and threw it at it and all we heard was glass shattering we busted out the car windows. The car instantly skirted and stopped in the middle of the street at this time I looked back as we are running, they slid the door open it was all Mexicans. With guns big guns at that, currently we are running, not to mention I couldn't hop certain gates, I could hop brick walls but at this moment it was a gate, and everyone hopped the gate but me. I was still stuck on the other side. My cousin turned back around and hopped back over to get me and helped me get over the gate. After we got over the gate, they were chasing us, so they hopped the gate too with guns and all. By it being night, it was really dark outside nobody knew where we were this was the first time in my life I was actually scared. I believed in my head that were going to be dead and gone and nobody would have known that we were in that ditch. We ran as far as we can down in the ditch and at this time, I started praying asking God to please get me out of this I'm not going to be bad anymore I was literally crying praying saying how I'm going to be a better person. After I got done praying, we ended up laying down in the ditch they couldn't see us but we saw them looking for us pointing their guns it was at least about a good 30 minutes that they were still looking for us, but we still stayed down we stayed there for a good hour until we didn't see or hear anyone. We ended up going back to the house and I ended up telling myself that this is not the life I want as a kid I had a real-life death scare I could have been murdered. When I got back to Compton I never looked back as far as doing dumb shit ever again I was only twelve years old and still had a lot to live for.

Chapter 9

Set Up

After I decided to be a better me, I still couldn't catch a break. I started to focus more on my talents and one of my talents was dancing, so I joined a well-known dance group which was Tommy the Clown out in Los Angeles Ca. I attended a battle zone that took place at world on wheels. It was super packed, it was crowded, people were getting frustrated. We were waiting a long time because other dance crews were showing up late, so the lines were super long. While we were waiting a big fight broke out and all I seen was cops and swat trucks pulling up hopping out with their full armor on as if it was the watts riot. So, they formed this line and next thing you know it was shots fired. And as for me, how it is on my block when you hear shots fire you run. So, I ran and me not knowing where I'm running too my only intentions is running away from where the shots were fired. I ran towards the police where they blocked all the cars at. All I know is I started getting beat by the police officers they were beating me with billy clubs and after they realized I was a kid they just stopped and let me go they didn't even try to help me they just started shooting toward the crowd that I ran from, they didn't know who was shooting all I know is I was trying to get away. As I started running, I collapsed my leg went out from all the beating that the police did and thank God for these two women that saw me, and they came and helped me, they dragged me and put me in their car. They let me use their phone and I called my grandmother and when she got to me, she took me to the hospital, and they examined me, and they wrapped my legs and told me to stay off of them. At this time, it reminded me of that near death experience that I had when I ran from the guys in the ditch, I was thirteen when this happened, I couldn't believe I experienced another one of them moments only this time I was innocent. I couldn't walk for two weeks and throughout my adult life I can still feel my leg dislocating from time to time.

Chapter 10

Solo

After dealing with childhood trauma and neglect also trying to find ways to escape my reality, I got into singing and song writing this is where I found my true passion because it allowed me to express myself and it changed the way that I think far as being out there ripping and running the streets. I was able to get somewhere to sit down and focus on my music. I started hanging around an older crowd when I was 16. This was my first time at a professional recording studio, and they didn't even charge me to use the studio. That was the first song that I wrote and recorded. I sang, and I rapped on that track, it was like therapy to me and at that moment that's when I knew what I wanted to do. After hearing myself when they played back my song, I knew I had potential. I told myself that I was going to pursue music and never give up on it. That's exactly what I did.

I was dating, so if I wasn't with my girl, it would be back to the studio creating more music. In the midst of that things became more serious with my girlfriend so I started focusing more on me and her you know how that goes. See I didn't hang with a group of friends I kept my circle small I didn't trust a lot of niggas because we all know how that can be too. I had a lot of associates but not a lot of friends just put it like that. I felt even more secure just being up under my girl she kept a nigga safe and kept me out of a lot of shit.

Chapter 11

Falling Deep in Love

From middle school sweethearts to high school sweethearts, I found myself still being with the same girl. My mind was already made up that this was the only girl that I wanted to be with and couldn't see myself without. I was in love deeply even though we went through minor setbacks, from us being together she would do this petty shit like breaking up with me and getting back with me, eventually we got past that.

A year went by, and we were expecting our first child with each other, she got pregnant, I was going on seventeen, but she was already seventeen, we were only 5 months apart. This was planned, it was not an accident, we both agreed on having kids and we knew exactly what we were doing. I think that I was more excited than she was because I wanted to be a dad. I believe I just wanted the family I never had which is a mom and dad living in the same household and raising their kids together, pretty much I wanted to be the one to break that cycle and that's the part that made me happy to be a dad. Everything started going good up until I sensed a jealous spirit on her mom. It was like she wanted her daughter's life far as how I was treating her daughter really good and spoiling her. Mind you were only kids, but I took really good care of her being by her side every step of the way I had two jobs, so she wasn't wanted for anything. Her mom started making it hard for her, far as not taking her around or being there for her throughout her pregnancy. She didn't take us anywhere, we had to get on buses just to get around. I had two jobs I worked at burger king and a woman clothing store so that's how I got around on the bus but that didn't stop me from making sure she had everything for her pregnancy. I did the whole baby shower, I brought all the clothes, everything the baby needed. I even made sure she had everything she craved while being pregnant.

One night I got a call from my girl. She was upset. She told me that she and her mom got into a physical fight, and she ended up kicking her out of the house, I couldn't believe what I was hearing not fighting while she was pregnant with my baby. Why would her mom even do that to her, but I wouldn't put it past her she always felt some type of way about her own daughter. It was late that night and I ended up getting a ride to her house and picked her up so she could come and stay with me and my granny while she finished her pregnancy.

Chapter 12

Domestic Violence

Now that she's finally moved in and settled, we prepared to get ready to have our baby. A few months later we were there having our first-born child, It was our first experience and she got upset with me and didn't want me in the room while she was having our daughter, I couldn't understand what her problem was but she told the doctors to make me leave out of the room I was so upset I missed out on the best part of my life me seeing my child being born, I didn't get to cut the umbilical cord. I still can't believe how she made me miss out on that. All I heard was my daughter finally made her grand entrance into this world. She was so beautiful she looked just like her mom she was a sky bright just like her mom. I didn't know after having my daughter her mom was going to change towards me, I sensed her attitude had changed towards me. I did everything that I was supposed to as a father, I never left her bedside. She breastfed the baby and for the times she didn't I was feeding my daughter her bottles and changing her diapers doing what I was supposed to while her mom was able to rest and get that time that she needed when she didn't have the baby in her care. So, I didn't understand where all the anger and the madness came from. Her attitude turned into anger and her anger turned into hate towards me. After months went by, she even became suicidal, it's like she always wanted to be physical. I remember one night when I went to work, she abused herself. She would beat herself and put bruises on herself to make it believe that I was putting my hands on her, and she was bright so the bruises would be there. When I would get off from work, I would pull up to my house and the police would be right there getting ready to arrest me for something that she made up in her head that I did, she really had a serious problem. There I was being arrested and the police took me to jail. After so many attempts of her doing this, it started to look suspicious to the cops, she kept doing the same thing over and over and she would hurt herself and call the police and of course they would come out and arrest me. She would even get to the point where she would come to my court dates and write a letter to the DA's office telling them that she did all these things to herself because she was mad at me. She had a cycle and kept repeating these same cycles. This one last time we got into it, I was just getting home from work, and she tried to pull some bullshit on me, don't get me wrong I reached my breaking point, she threw a glass vase at my face, and she busted my eye open. I didn't hit her with a closed fist, but I smashed her fucking head against the wall and that's when I called the police. When the police arrived that's when they knew that she had a problem and instead of them arresting me, they took her to the mental hospital. They put her on a 48 hour hold she stayed for a few days. After they released her, she had to come back home with me everything was going well until she started back getting violent with me, we kept getting into fist fights and that's when my grandma had enough, she ended up kicking us out and it was like one in the morning. We packed up our baby and had to get a hotel for the night. The next day we went and applied for the county so we could get their homeless assistance to where they helped us pay for our hotel expenses. We even got our first apartment and they paid for our down payment. We had our first apartment together and during this time I thought everything was going to be different for us because now we didn't have grandma to depend on, we were officially on our own. Everything had gotten worse. She said that she wasn't going to stop, and that she was going to ruin my life even if it was going to sacrifice our daughter, she used to do random shit to my daughter like scream at her just to get under my skin, yelling at her saying she wish she never had her all to make me upset. I used to be pissed off, but I had to play it safe because I didn't want her doing anything that was going to hurt my daughter. So, I ended up staying and she ended up pregnant again. We had a boy I figured at least with him things were going to get better but yet that still didn't change nothing, I was so happy to have my first son I had a little me, I couldn't wait to have that father and son bond with him, raise him to be different than I was but because of my situation I believed that she hated me and that we weren't going to be that family that I wanted us to be in the very beginning. Instead, I wanted to leave her, but I couldn't because I didn't want my kids in her care.

Chapter 13

Custody Battle

Back in 2011 I had enough, I finally kicked her out of my house and told her not to come back. She left and stayed gone for months and it was just me and the kids. With me working so much trying to juggle my job and my music career and being a father at the same time I really didn't have the help or daycare to help me support my kids so I ended up calling my grandmother to come and pick up my kids just to stay with her for a little while until I figured out my situation or what I was going to do next. Months went by, next thing you know the police were at my house with paperwork, asking where the kids were, that's the day that I found out that I was being served with custody paperwork, something that I didn't have any knowledge about. I ended up having to give my kids up to the mom. From then on that's when I went and filed my own papers to fight and get my kids back. We went back and forth doing this custody battle from joint custody to full custody for the next ten years. It started to become really petty, she ended up moving and didn't let me know that she was moving, and she hid me from my kids for a whole year. I didn't have any contact or any whereabouts. That's when she took advantage of the situation and she lied and told my kids that I was in prison. During the year I went and filed for an abduction because she was not following the court ordered papers, I ended up contacting the police to continue to fight for my kids so they could find them. I was stressed out, I cried numerous nights wondering where my kids were. hoping that they were ok and that she was treating them good. I would go and search different cities where I knew that she would be and that's when I ended up finding them. When I got to one of the locations, I knew she was there, but she didn't open up the door, she turned off all of the lights, she even told the kids to be quit, but I did not leave I stayed and even called the police to come out. When the police came out, they couldn't even do anything about the situation even when I showed them my court papers. I was upset but I was happy that I found them at the same time.

The following day I went to find out what school they were in. When I got the information, I went up to their schools and I checked them out. There was another court date set in place and they ended up turning the kids back over to the mom and gave us joint custody. After her doing all of what she did by hiding the kids for a whole year I feel the courts didn't do anything about it and they still showed her favor. I was hurt about it.

Chapter 14

Single Father

My daughter and my son started getting a little older now, they were becoming aware of what was going on between me and their mom, far as how they were going back and forth from my house to hers. My kid's mom continued to do what she wanted to do and not go by court orders and still tried to keep the kids away from me. She started to not answer the phones and didn't let them call me. They used to get whooped when they would ask her can they call me.

One day they snuck and called me on the phone, their mom caught them on the phone with me I heard the phone drop, I heard all of the yelling and screaming, and I heard my daughter say get off of me "Why you punch me in my face. I just heard a lot of tumbling as if they were fighting so I immediately hung up the phone and called the police. At this time, I was in a different city from my kids. The police got there and talked to the mom, they didn't arrest the mom, they ended up letting her go. The following morning, I woke up and my kids were at my front door in their pajamas. They had no shoes on, and no jackets, the weather was bad at the time it was really cold outside, I thought it was a movie. My kids were at my doorstep, they were crying, and my daughter's neck was all scratched up. I called the police, the detectives came out and talked to my kids they also took pictures of their bruises, at this point it had gotten serious because my daughter and my son said that their mom threatened to kill them in their sleep with a shot gun. She told my son that she was going to shoot him in his private area, she didn't exactly say where she was going to shoot my daughter.

After they investigated, they ended up getting a search warrant for my kid's mom's house. When they went in, they found the shot gun loaded and ready to go. They immediately arrested her and set another court date. She ended up bailing out, at this point it was too late she lost all custody to seeing the kids, that's physical, and joint custody she had no contact whatsoever. She lost it all. The more my kids got interviewed, the more things came out that I couldn't even believe. My son came out and expressed that he was getting sexually abused. She used to randomly ask him to see his private area and when he got in trouble, she would tell him to get naked and whoop his private area only. When I heard my son express what he was going through with his mom, I broke down and cried. I also found out that my kids' mom was encouraging my daughter to have a boyfriend which led her to losing her virginity at her mom house, and that broke my soul when I heard my daughter side of the story, she was actually crying when she had to tell me that. This is why I wanted full custody to begin with so I could have prevented any of this from happening to them. The mom allowed them to do everything as if they were her friends, she even smoked and drank with my daughter by peer pressure. Both of my kids are smart, healthy, intelligent, and talented. Since they have been with me, they have gotten caught up with their grades, which is amazing. I feel with me they are able to be kids and not have to grow up so fast by being adults at a young age. I'm a fun father but I also have structure at the same time.

After a year of me having my kids getting adapted to how I do things and how I run my household far as keeping them on track and keeping them focus on school just doing all the right things and them getting used to the lifestyle a healthy lifestyle at that. I found out a year later that my kids' mom was contacting my daughter to try and manipulate her and brainwash her also made her change her mind about living with me. In due time it actually worked, my daughter ran away, and they planned the whole thing. It was my kid's mom and her mother; they are the ones who picked my daughter up.

I wasn't aware at the time so being a concerned father I put out an APB on her and shared it to my social media asking my family and friends to share the info if they see or heard anything about her whereabouts. I found out in a few months that it was the mom and the grandma who was behind everything. I kind of put two and two together because my daughter doesn't socialize with a lot of people, and she didn't have any friends like that.

I understand why she left in a sense because I have structure in my household and any teen would go where they could do whatever they want. Being a single father is not easy, but I wouldn't trade it for nothing. For any father out there that gets in a situation like this I advise them to have a lot of patience and try not to break, because life has its way of showing up unexpectedly and when it happen to you all you have to do is man up and fight against all odds and not let nothing come between your man hood or take anything less from you. every man deserves to be a part of their child life and I'm speaking on the fathers that truly wants to be there, but the mother is making it hard for them not too. Just keep fighting cause at the end of the day the truth will always reveal itself.

Chapter 15

Gotta Do Something

After all I've gone through, I managed to stay consistent with my music career. I decided to take it a little further. Even though the last ten years have been rough and hard I still had the fire in me to keep on going. I started networking with other people who were on the same level as me or even higher than me, the people that were going to help push me to another level. I continued to put in the work, I started from the bottom, and I stayed very consistent. My name started to ring bells and I started to become known. I developed a small team, with people that I have known over the last ten years. I had my camera man, my own security, and a videographer, and everywhere that I went they went. I believe out of every artist in my city I'm the only one that showed up everywhere with my team. My name became popular off that alone, not to mention my fashion, I had my own style but most importantly I had talent.

I started to make more music and create the videos to go with it. I had to do something because I knew that my kids were watching, not only were they watching I also involved them too. I didn't have that much guidance in the industry, or anyone to hold my hand but I did my best to make a name for myself. I was still working my 9-5, I took care of my household with that, and I put the rest into my music. I would rent out little bars to throw events for myself to get my name out there. I would pay for my own marketing expenses, even then I didn't make more money I lost more money than what I put in. That was the sacrifice that I was willing to take because I took my music career serious cause It was my dream ever since I was a kid.

Chapter 16

The Industry

All the work that I have been putting in over the years, it finally started paying off for me. Yung Muusik, the name that I've made for my self has finally made it. The industry also knows me as "The Red-Carpet King", which I find funny but at the same time true. I have been invited to every event that you could think of and listed as VIP. I could now say that I am living out my dream, that dream that I had when I was a kid to now is my reality. I might not be where I want to be but I'm not far from it. I'm just happy that I'm not where I used to be.

Sometimes when I'm in these rooms I still can't believe it because some of the artists that I've grown up listening to know my name and my music. I have met so many big-time celebrities and I've learned over the years. "Who you surround yourself with is who you become. Throughout my journey I decided to help others to find their way in the industry that didn't have the help or resources like me. It's all a blessing to be where I am today in my life and working towards a bigger dream for myself, being that example to others just like me, and inspiring them to do whatever they put their mind to. It wasn't an easy journey, but it was well worth it. I have been talked down on, lied on, talked about and people even doubted me, and they still do doubt me. I have helped people that even turned their back on me due to jealousy and envy because they didn't have what it takes to do half of the things that I did to get me where I'm at. I guess they thought it was a free ride to reach levels but there aint no short cuts in life, it's all-hard work and dedication. I grinded, I hustled day in and day out and it wasn't no stopping me. What I did do is I stopped hanging with people that saw me as a competition, all I wanted to do was help people so instead of pulling people in and getting that backlash. I decided to start my own nonprofit organization which stands out in my community called "YungPowerFoundation".Our mission is to help the youth and I give back. Our nonprofit does Christmas giveaways, backpack giveaways and food drives. I've always given back to my community and I'm going to continue to do what I do in the most humble way, I'm forever grateful and I thank God for it all. Here is some knowledge that I want to put out there, "in order to get to your dreams just remember that you have to go through the bad to get to the good.

About The Author

BIO

Yung Muusik, the R&B recording artist, singer-songwriter, rapper, and entrepreneur, is creating a buzz in the music industry with his unique style and soulful vocals. Born and raised in Compton, California, Yung Muusik's music is heavily influenced by the urban culture and life experiences of his hometown. Yung Muusik is set to release his highly anticipated album titled "Universal Love," which is expected to be a huge success. The album features an edgy and insightful sound that is certain to attract fans from around the world. Yung Muusik's authentic and real approach to life and music is evident in his songwriting, making him stand out as a genuine artist.

Yung Muusik's latest single, "Boo Thang," is out now on Vevo, YouTube, and all digital platforms, and the official music video is also available to watch. The single showcases Yung Muusik's unique sound and personality and is just a taste of what fans can expect from his upcoming album.

Aside from his music career, Yung Muusik has also started a nonprofit called "YoungPowerFoundation", in partnership with Kween Elevation, to give back to the community.

Yung Muusik has performed at numerous venues, including The Improv, Club Bliss, Cal State University, and many more. With his stunning vocal displays and captivating performances, he has gained a dedicated fan base and is poised for even greater success.

Investors and business partners are proud to present this rising R&B

Yung Muusik & Industry Friends

I will continue to shine and let my hard work and dedication speak for me, and for every room that I enter into, I will always be myself and most importantly I'll remain humbled as my blessings flow and allow God to get the glory out of my life.

Yung Muusik & Family

I stumbled on these photographs, they kind of made me laugh, it took me way back...

"Back Down Memory Lane"!

There's No "Hood" Like Fatherhood

Pursuit of Success

In the pursuit of success, there will always be those who doubt you, those who try to bring you down, and those who say you can't make it. But remember, the path to success is rarely easy. It is paved with challenges, setbacks, and moments of doubt. Yet, it is precisely during these tough times that your true strength shines through. Ignore the naysayers, the skeptics, and the critics. Stay true to your dreams and aspirations. Stay focused on your goals, no matter how hard things get. Believe in yourself, your abilities, and your potential to overcome any obstacle that comes your way. Remember, success is not defined by the words of others, but by your own actions, determination, and resilience. Look to role models like I Yung Muusik, who faced similar challenges and emerged victorious through hard work and unwavering belief in themselves. So, keep pushing forward, keep striving for greatness, and keep believing in your journey. The road to success may be tough, but with persistence, dedication, and a strong belief in yourself, you can achieve anything you set your mind to. You have what it takes to succeed – now go out there and make it happen!"

I stand before you today not just as an individual, but as a testament to the resilience and strength that lies within each of us. My journey has been one marked by hardship, challenges, and obstacles that seemed insurmountable at times. Growing up, I faced adversity, and as a single father, I carried the weight of responsibility on my shoulders. In the midst of my struggles, I found myself in an abusive relationship with the mother of my children. Despite the pain and turmoil, I held on to a glimmer of hope and faith that there was a greater purpose for my life. I refused to let my circumstances define me or dictate my future. I truly believe that God had plans for me, plans that involved not just my own success, but a deeper mission to motivate and inspire others. Each trial I faced was a steppingstone towards a greater calling - to be a source of blessing and encouragement to those around me. Today, I stand before you as living proof that no matter how challenging life may seem, there is always a way forward. I fought for what I wanted in life, not just for myself, but for my children and for all those who have faced similar struggles. My experiences have shaped me into a beacon of hope, a reminder that resilience, faith, and perseverance can lead us through the darkest of times. My story is a testament to the fact that we are stronger than our circumstances, and that our past does not define our future. I urge each of you to hold on to hope, to believe in your own strength, and to know that there is a purpose in every trial we face. May my journey serve as a reminder that no matter what life throws our way, we have the power to rise above, to inspire others, and to be a blessing to those around us. Thank you.

Yung Muusik Award Winnings

I went from being homeless to winning Awards alongside legends that I've watched growing up on TV.

Yung Power Foundation

I went from being homeless, helpless to helping others/ families and in all communities with my foundation called Yung Power Foundation. This is a major blessing.

Consistency is Key

To get to a place that you've never been, you must put in the work and be consistent, don't ever let nothing or nobody stop you, "grind like never before and let your light shine. Do it for you and if you have kids do it for them because they are looking up to you and they are watching you be the number one example in their life. Whoever else doesn't like it, they will adapt, or they will fall off, either way it goes never give up because consistency is key to all the unlocked doors that cross your path.

Believe

There will come a time in your life where nobody will believe in you more than you will ever believe in yourself. You must want what you want for you more than others. I can strongly say this because when you do reach that point in your life where you can finally see yourself winning and when you look back the applause that you have been waiting for won't be what you thought that it would. Always remember that a lot of people won't clap for you when you win so long as you clap for yourself there will not be any regrets and you will be glad that you did. Always believe in yourself.

Keep The Faith

Faith will open doors that nobody could shut. Through success Faith is one of the most important things on your journey, without faith how can you be able to see the blessings on the other side. Keep the faith and no matter how hard it gets, never allow yourself to give up. Once you can keep the faith you can get through anything, and you can unlock any door. I am a witness to have keeping the faith works. When I felt like giving up, I always reminded myself that as long as I have faith, I'm going to make it. Anything is possible with prayer, keeping the faith and trusting the process.

Thank You

Thank You to everyone who's been really down with me on my journey, from me becoming an Artist all the way up to me becoming an Author. I truly appreciate it from the bottom of my heart it feels really good to know that I have support and the people that have been supporting me still in my corner and not only do you all support me you believe in me as well. This is to those who really have my back I pray that you continue to be blessed and what you poured into me it comes back to you even double. The love doesn't go unnoticed and thank you again and again.

www.ingramcontent.com/pod-product-compliance
Lightning Source LLC
Chambersburg PA
CBHW071225160426
43196CB00012B/2415